The Missing Telescope

by Cas Lester
Illustrated by Emma Levey

OXFORD
UNIVERSITY PRESS

In this story ...

Pip Squeak

Kit Bags

Pip and Kit run *Finders Squeakers* – a lost and found agency. They help return lost things to their owners.

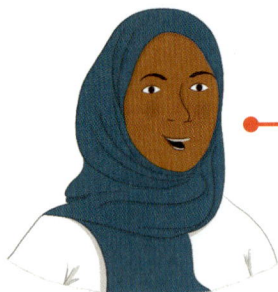

• •

Farah Salah

Chapter 1
A new adventure

Pip was reading a message from the famous explorer Farah Salah.

"Farah is about to set off on a new adventure," Pip told Kit excitedly. "She wants our help!"

Fish Fans

"Our help?" asked Kit. "Does she want us to go with her?"

"Not exactly," Pip said, with a laugh. "She wants us to find her telescope."

Pip explained that Farah had been flying in her hot-air balloon when she accidentally dropped her telescope over the side.

She'd sent Pip and Kit a photo of the telescope. It was made of brass and looked old.

"It's her <u>personal</u> favourite," said Pip.

<u>Personal</u> things are things that belong to you. How would you feel if you lost something that was your <u>personal</u> favourite?

Farah had also sent a map showing where she had dropped the telescope.

"If we have a map, it should be easy-peasy to find the telescope," said Kit.

"Not really," Pip replied. "She dropped it in the ocean."

"Oh," said Kit.

Kit scratched his head. "How are we going to search for something under the sea?" he asked.

Pip looked around the workshop. "Hmm. I <u>shall</u> have to make something special."

"I'll help," said Kit eagerly.

I <u>shall</u> means I will. Imagine you are Pip. Explain what you are going to make. You could start with: *I <u>shall</u> ...*

There was a lot of clanking and clattering, banging and bashing. Pip and Kit worked all day and most of the night.

Finally …

"Ta da!" Pip said. "One submarine!"

The submarine had a metal detector. It also had a super-strong grabber.

Chapter 2
Under the waves

Early the next morning, Pip and Kit packed some sandwiches. Then they set off for Tailton harbour with the submarine. They tied it to a trailer, which rattled noisily behind their motorbike.

At the harbour, they clambered into the submarine. Kit closed the hatch with a loud *CLUNK*. As they sank under the waves, the engine rumbled loudly. The propeller started to spin.

They set off at full speed.

Later …

Pip stared out of the thick glass window.

"Look at all the fish," she squeaked. "Aren't they amazing?"

"Amazing," Kit mumbled. He listened nervously to the noises the submarine was making. "Being underwater isn't <u>natural</u> for cats," he thought.

How do you think Kit feels about being underwater? Where do you think is a more <u>natural</u> place for a cat to be?

11

Pip checked Farah's map. "We should be nearly there."

Just then, the metal detector started bleeping.

"Maybe the metal detector has found the telescope!" Kit said excitedly.

However, it wasn't the telescope. It was just a rusty anchor.

Not long afterwards, they saw an old shipwreck.
BLEEP went the metal detector.

Pip quickly steered the submarine close to the shipwreck. She sighed. The metal detector had found the ship's bell.

Then the metal detector bleeped again.

Pip held her breath … was this it?

Chapter 3
The telescope

This time it was the telescope! It was half buried between some large rocks.

"We've found it!" Pip cried.

"Yes, but how are we going to get it?" asked Kit.

"This is how ..." said Pip. She pressed some buttons, and the grabber stretched out from the front of the submarine.

Pip pressed some more buttons, but she struggled to get a grip on the telescope. It kept slipping through the grabber's claws.

Suddenly, a large octopus swam up and clung on to the submarine, blocking the window.

Pip couldn't see anything. "Out of the way!" she said crossly.

The octopus finally drifted away, and Pip managed to grab the telescope.

"At last!" she cried.

"Let's go home," said Kit.

Pip turned the submarine around.

Just then, a dark shape loomed beside them. It was a <u>massive</u>, hungry-looking shark!

Kit gulped. "Uh oh."

Imagine you are Pip or Kit in their submarine and you see a <u>massive</u> shark. What would you say? What would you do?

17

Chapter 4
Shark chase!

Pip squealed. Quickly, she switched the controls to super speed. The engine roared and water whooshed behind them.

The submarine shot forward, but the shark swam after it.

"Faster!" wailed Kit.

WHOOSH!

Pip called out, "Hold on tight, Kit!" She yanked the controls to one side.

WHOOSH! The submarine shot off to the left. Then ... *WHOOSH* ... it zigzagged to the right.

Kit glanced out the window. "The shark is getting closer!"

Up ahead, they saw the old shipwreck they'd passed earlier.

"Quick, hide in there!" cried Kit.

Pip steered the submarine through a hole in the side of the ship.

The shark was much too big to follow them.

"That was close," said Pip with a sigh.

"Too close," Kit added.

They waited a long time, until the shark gave up and finally swam away. Pip <u>cautiously</u> steered the submarine out of the shipwreck.

Why did Pip steer the submarine <u>cautiously</u>? What was she afraid of?

The next day …

Pip was reading *The Daily Newts*.

There was a picture of Farah Salah in her hot-air balloon on the front page.

"I'm glad we found the telescope," said Pip. "It says here that Farah is very happy to have it back."

The Daily Newts

Explorer Recovers Lost Telescope

"Maybe we could go on an adventure with Farah one day?" said Pip. "What do you think, Kit?"

Kit didn't answer. He was curled up in his bed snoring loudly, still tired out from their underwater adventure.

Read and discuss

Read and talk about the following questions.

Page 5: Can you describe your <u>personal</u> favourite toy or book?

Page 7: Imagine you are Farah planning an adventure. Talk about where you're going to go. You could say, *First, I <u>shall</u>* …

Page 11: The sea is a <u>natural</u> environment. Can you name any other <u>natural</u> environments?

Page 15: Can you think of a time when it was a <u>struggle</u> to do something?

Page 17: Which other animals might you describe as <u>massive</u>?

Page 21: Why do you need to be <u>cautious</u> when crossing a road? What do you do to keep safe?